Conscious
DREAMER

Conscious DREAMER

Connect with the power of your dreams & live your best life

Tree Carr

Illustrated by Hello Marine

First published in the UK in 2021 by
Leaping Hare Press
An imprint of The Quarto Group
The Old Brewery, 6 Blundell Street
London N7 9BH, United Kingdom
T (0)20 7700 6700 F (0)20 7700 8066
www.QuartoKnows.com

British Library Cataloguing-in-Publication Data
A catalogue record for this book is available from the British Library

ISBN: 978-0-7112-6121-1

This book was conceived, designed and produced by
Leaping Hare Press
58 West Street, Brighton BN1 2RA, United Kingdom
Publisher Richard Green
Art Director Paileen Currie
Editorial Director Jennifer Barr
Commissioning Editor Chloe Murphy
Designer Sally Bond

Printed in China

10 9 8 7 6 5 4 3 2 1

Contents

Introduction
We all dream

We all dream. Despite our differences in culture, age, gender and beliefs, we are all linked by the mysterious, transcendent and surreal nature of our dreams.

In the modernized world, it can feel like we no longer dream. Many of us have adopted more conscious ways of living in response to modern obstacles, but most of the changes we make are in our waking lives. This book will teach you how you can embrace and reconnect with yourself and your dreams, and make the most of your magical dreaming hours.

The great potential of dreams

Your consciousness doesn't stop as soon as you put your head down on your pillow. You spend about a third of your life asleep and dreaming, and your consciousness can still carry through in that state. That's 25 years of your life of untapped potential!

There are countless examples of scientific breakthroughs, creative works of art and literature, and eureka moments that have come through in dreams. Dreams not only serve as muses for creativity, but are visual playgrounds in which we can problem solve.

Lucid dreaming – the art of becoming conscious within the dream state – can be used for personal transformation, while pre-cognitive (psychic) dreams can give you prompts and warnings to help you in your waking life. The beauty of your dreams is that you receive what's right for YOU. So whoever you are, you can learn to use your dreams to trigger breakthrough moments and transform your life.

How to use this book

This book is designed to give you the necessary tools to become more connected with your dreamworlds and therefore bring more inspiration, guidance, healing, creativity and magic into your waking life. Over the next 30 days, I will guide you through a conscious dreaming practice which will help you to build new habits around sleep and dreaming.

Embark on this adventure when the timing feels intuitively right for you. As a conscious dreamer, you will be embracing your dreams through a series of fun activities on a daily and nightly basis. I'll be here throughout your journey as your personal dream guide.

Each activity is labelled with a little symbol to indicate at what time of the day it is to be carried out. Use this key to help you see timings at a glance:

KEY

 Morning activity

 Daytime activity

 Nightime activity

 Bedtime ritual (see page 33)

 Dream tea ritual (see page 44)

 Reality check (see page 60)

 W.I.L.D. meditation (see page 66)

 Share on social media

Join the #ConsciousDreamer community

For each day, I've included an optional social media activity for you to have fun with. Join in with these when the mood takes you; they can help you interact with other dreamers and document your journey even more. Dream sharing is a hugely important part of your conscious dreaming practice, so you can use the hashtag #ConsciousDreamer each time you post to help you find and connect with other conscious dreamers. There's no limit to the amount of insight, fun and support to be gained by embracing and becoming part of a dream community!

What you need for your journey

Practical things you will need:

A pen
Scissors
Tape or glue
Paints, colour pencils or markers
A notebook to use as your dream journal
Access to a printer (optional)

Disclaimer

On day 6 I will be asking you to research and procure some dream herbs and plants to help enhance your conscious dreaming experience. Please ensure that you thoroughly research any herbs or plants before ingesting them, and if you are pregnant or have any allergies or health concerns, avoid this activity altogether. It is always best to consult a doctor first if you have any concerns, and I have provided an alternative activity that will be just as beneficial if you choose not to partake in consuming dream herbs or plants.

Your completed body of dreamwork

Over the next 30 days you will be engaging in regular rituals and activities that will help activate your dreams, such as writing, dream mapping and sharing, meditating and building a dream altar.

Each activity will help trigger more vivid and meaningful dreams and help you to understand them more deeply.

At the end of these 30 days you will have accumulated a month's dreamwork: a body of work that you can use as a foundation or 'sketchbook' to help achieve the goal you set yourself at the beginning of this journey. Whether your intent is to explore your subconcious creativity, try your hand at creative writing, or simply to get to know yourself better, the content of your journey will help you to spark your imagination, and achieve your goals.

PART I:
Falling

Set Your Intent

Welcome, conscious dreamer!

Today is the first day of your 30-day journey to becoming better connected with your dreams. It will enable you to form new habits and get to know the side of yourself that holds so much untapped potential. You'll be guided through a variety of activities, and over the next month you will see your ability to connect to your dreams evolve and improve.

Dreaming goals

It's important to begin your 30-day journey with an intention – a goal. Perhaps you're an artist and you'd like your dreams to help inspire new ideas for artwork, for example, or maybe you're shy and you'd like your dreams to help you be more assertive. Wherever you are in your life, and whatever your passions or everyday activities, you can use your dreams to help enrich your waking life experiences. It simply starts with intent.

Over the next 30 days, your intent will be the thread that weaves through from start to finish. Your original intent, which you'll fix on in today's four activities, will evolve over your journey. You will finish this book both with a sense of accomplishment and connection, and a body of work achieved through the direct experience of your dreams.

Get started: ruminate and reflect

Before you start, settle yourself comfortably. Then concentrate on your goal: what you want to achieve. What would you like your dreams to help you with? When you are thinking, try to connect with your intuition, the 'gut feeling' within you that gives you an inner voice about what you really want or need. Often this may be linked with your life's passions.

Fill out the questions on the next page to help your rumination process and pick one or more of the feelings listed in the cloud to describe how each answer makes you feel. Emotions are powerful energy and they're an important aspect of setting your intent, so you need to be aware of them when they pop up. Dreams, after all, are the realms of your unconscious mind and that's where most of your emotions live, so to help you set the best goal for the next 30 days, pay attention to both the positive and negative emotions that crop up.

Take each question and try to express the thinking process behind your answer.

For example, 'My passion is helping animals. This makes me feel happy and inspired. It also makes me feel sad because there is so much destruction happening in the natural world that directly affects the welfare of animals.'

Happy

Sad

Excited

Confused

Neutral

Anxious

Fearful

Inspired

Bored

Self-critical

Other

What are my life goals?

....
....
....
....
....

What changes do I want to bring in my life?

....
....
....
....
....

What are my personal obstacles?

....
....
....
....
....

What would I like to achieve over the next 30 days?

....
....
....
....
....

✸ Set your intention

My intention and goal for the next 30 days is:

....

....

....

....

....

....

....

....

....

....

....

....

....

....

....

Now sit in quiet reflection for a minute or two.
   Then recite your statement of intent ten times out loud, and sense the positive feeling/emotion in your body as you speak it. You may even feel that your positive emotion grows as you repeat your statement of intent.

 Share a picture of your book with some words about how you feel at the beginning of your 30-day journey.

🌙 Recite your intention

Before you fall asleep in bed tonight, recite your statement of intent ten times in your mind (you don't have to say it aloud), and feel the positive emotions associated with that intent.

Tonight is the first night of your journey: let your intentions and dreams be activated! See you tomorrow morning for day 2.

Dream journalling

Keeping a record of your nightly dreams is what will trigger the biggest changes as you evolve as a conscious dreamer. I have asked you to use a notebook as your dream journal, but there are many ways in which you can record your dreams.

The key is to get the dream out of your mind and into your waking reality in some form or another, before it is lost and forgotten. Your dreams are ALWAYS communicating with you – not recording them is like missing the memo.

Dream journalling is a simple tool that helps us become more consciously aware of our inner worlds, and once you begin a regular dedicated dream-recording practice, you will begin to understand what it is to be a conscious dreamer. Dreamwork will become fun, creative and revealing.

To record your dreams, you need a disciplined on-waking routine, and a method of recording that suits you. You might like to record them in your designated journal, type them out on your phone, message them to a friend, record yourself recounting the dream, film yourself, draw a sketch or picture, or a mixture of the above. Just make sure you have what you need nearby, so you can reach for it as soon as you wake.

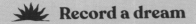 **Record a dream**

If you have a fresh dream to hand, try recording it in your new dream journal. If you're struggling to remember your dream, you can practise recording a dream you remember from the past.

To record your dream in your journal:

- Start by writing out the full date.
- Now write an account of the dream. Write with a flowing stream of consciousness. Your mission should be to get as many details written down as possible before you lose the dream.
- Record how you felt in the dream. Your emotional response within the dream is one of the biggest clues you will receive for decoding it.
- Next, record the setting of the dream, in as much detail as you can.
- Note any abstractions or less straightforward aspects of your dream. For example, 'I found a wounded bird on the ground. For some reason it reminded me of my mother.' It is important to note these details, as abstractions can contain big clues that will help you to interpret your dream later on.
- Finally, document the sensory aspects of your dream. Include any details of colours, textures, shapes, sounds, aromas, or physical actions. These can be important symbols that can assist in dream interpretation.

 Share a photo of your dream journal with some words about the dream you have just recorded.

🌙 Put your dream journal by your bedside

Before you settle down for the night, ensure that your journal or other method of recording your dream is nearby. You will need to record your dream as soon as you wake up in the morning.

🌙 Revisit your intention

Before you fall asleep, recite your statement of intent ten times in your mind, and feel the positive emotions associated with that intent.

Have an inspired dreamtime. Your dream memory recall should begin improving nightly. See you tomorrow morning for day 3!

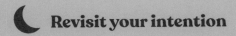

Understand Your Sleep Cycles

Good morning conscious dreamer!

I hope that your first night of dreaming was an engaging one. Today you're going to practise some activities that will look at your own sleep cycles and the kind of sleep patterns you have, because understanding what goes on biologically every night when your head rests on your pillow is a huge help in cultivating your conscious dreaming practice.

🌟 Record your dreams

But before you begin today's activities, record your dreams from last night in your journal using the guidelines from day 2. If you can't remember any dreams, simply write down your impressions, feelings, or thoughts upon awakening.

Stages of sleeping

Now you've had the first few nights' sleep of your 30-day journey, it's the perfect time to go over your sleep cycles. Understanding your sleep cycle will also help you to achieve a lucid dream, which is a dream in which you are aware, conscious and in control. There will be more about this in week two.

When you sleep, you pass through five stages. You can visualize it like a dive in the ocean. As you dive, you pass through different depths – the five stages of sleep. Each stage can last between 5 and 15 minutes. When you get to the bottom of the ocean – deep sleep – you stay there for a while, then begin to rise to the surface again. You then repeat the dive back down again. Each deep dive is one complete sleep cycle, which takes an average of 90–110 minutes to complete, and you may go through as many as six cycles in a full night's sleep.

Let's have a look at the different stages:

1 Dozy

This is the transitional state where you drift in and out of consciousness. This threshold is called the hypnagogic state. During it, many of us experience the twitching of our limbs or a feeling that we're falling, either of which can cause us to jolt awake. It's a state in which a lot of interesting phenomena go on. If you can train yourself to stay conscious and to observe them, you'll start to see dreams forming, clips of random scenes or faces, geometrical shapes, patterns, light, or colours. Sometimes you may even hear sounds like snippets of music or conversation.

2 Light sleep

During this phase of your sleep cycle, your heart rate begins to slow down, your core body temperature decreases, your eye movement stops and your brain waves slow down.

3 Deep sleep

Deeper sleep than stage two. Brainwaves shift into slower mode.

4 Deeper sleep

This is the phase in which you go into deep, restorative sleep. This makes you feel rested and keeps you healthy. It's really difficult to wake someone up from this sleep stage.

5 REM sleep

This is the phase of sleep in which you dream. 'REM' refers to Rapid Eye Movement; during this stage of the sleep cycle, your eyes move rapidly in different directions under your closed eyelids. During the REM phase your brain is as active as it is when you are awake. When you wake from REM sleep, it's called the hypnopompic state and you will usually experience lingering, vivid imagery from your dreams.

What kind of sleeper are you?

Circle one or more of the following:

Light   Deep   Restless

Restful   Other

 # Drawing your sleep cycle

Draw a visual representation of what your sleep cycle looks like to you, below. Perhaps it looks like crashing waves in the ocean, a wide-eyed owl, or a pebble sinking to the bottom of a pond. Get imaginative and just draw whatever springs to your mind!

 Take a photo of your drawing and share some words about what your sleeping patterns are like.

☾ Repeat your intention

Before you settle down to your third night's sleep, recite your statement of intent ten times in your mind, and feel the positive emotions associated with that intent.

When you've affirmed your intentions it's time to observe your hypnagogic state:

- Lie comfortably on your back in bed
- Relax your body
- Observe your body relaxing into heavy sensation
- Resist the urge to roll over and cuddle up – remain still and stationary on your back
- Focus your attention on the black backdrop of your closed eyes, as though it were a darkened movie cinema screen
- Continue to observe the movie cinema screen, waiting for the film to start
- Observe anything you notice visually
- Draw your attention to the thoughts or sounds in your mind, as if you were listening to a radio station
- Focus on listening to those thoughts or sounds
- Bring your attention back to your closed eyelids – the movie screen – and observe any visual content
- Then bring your attention back to your mind's sounds – the radio station – and listen to the content
- Practise going back and forth between the two – you may find you can do both at once.

☾ On waking on day 4

Tomorrow morning as you wake up, you're going to observe the threshold state between sleeping and waking: your hypnopompic state. As you feel yourself coming up to the surface from your dreams and sleep, observe what's happening to you. First thing tomorrow, write down your impressions upon awakening.

Tonight is the third night of your journey: let your intentions evolve and your dream experience be an inspiring one! I'll see you in the morning for day 4.

Improve Your Sleep Hygiene

Good morning conscious dreamer! I hope that your dreaming was active last night and that you were able to notice your hypnagogic state as you fell asleep. Don't worry too much if you didn't have an experience the first time around – you'll be practising every night throughout this journey.

One of the most important foundations to becoming a conscious dreamer is to look at all of the jobs and habits you take on before going to bed, and to improve them to ensure you sleep as well as possible. If your sleep hygiene is poor, you won't sleep as well or be so connected to your dreams, and poor sleep can take its toll on your health.

Record your waking and dreaming activity

Before you begin today's activities, record your dreams from last night in your dream journal.

Observe yourself waking

Before you slept last night, I prompted you to observe your awakening state. Record your waking experience in your dream journal, below your dream.

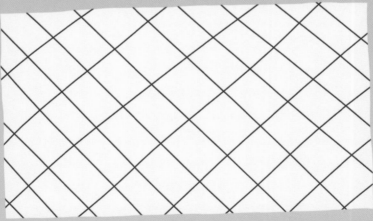

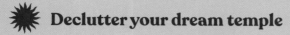 **Declutter your dream temple**

You should look at your bedroom as your dream temple.
For the next four weeks and beyond, this is your dedicated
space for good sleep and more connected dreaming.
Doing a spring clean will help shift up the stale energy of
unnecessary clutter. A good rule of thumb when decluttering
is to ask: 'Does this object have anything to do with sleep or
dreams?' If the answer is no, then put it in another room.

Declutter

Tidy up, moving any piles of clothes, books and so on
elsewhere. Get rid of any items that remind you of work and
remove screens if possible. If you only have a small space,
turn all screens off before you go to bed.

Clean

You already wash your bedding and nightwear, but to make
the surroundings as inviting as possible, you should clean the
less obvious parts too. Give the room a good weekly dust
and vacuum, under as well as around the bed, and turn the
mattress regularly.

✸ Consider the following and commit to making changes if necessary

Take some time to reflect on your typical bedtime experience. Do you often find yourself kept awake by light, noise or discomfort? Consider the suggestions below and think about what changes you could make to improve your sleeping environment.

Light and noise

Too much light in the room at night can prevent you from getting a solid sleep cycle. The same can be said for disruptive noises.

Check out whether you have the best curtains or blinds, and whether light from outside intrudes. If you find the light often disturbs you, wearing an eye mask can help.

Consider the noise levels from outside, and whether they disturb you. Soft silicone earplugs are comfortable to wear and can really help.

Your bed

Choosing the right mattress should be taken more seriously than choosing a car – it's the most important element when it comes to good-quality sleep. If your existing one really isn't comfortable, you may need to think about replacing it. If this isn't an option, a soft mattress topper could help. You spend a third of your life asleep and the quality of your sleep affects your life, as well as your dreams!

Your bedding

Check the comfort of your bed linen, duvets and pillows. Ensure they're the right weight, ideally made from natural fibres, and avoid noisy or clashing patterns: your bed linen should look as well as feel soothing.

 Share a photo of your newly decluttered dream temple.

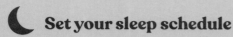 Set your sleep schedule

According to the National Sleep Foundation, adults typically need between seven and nine hours of sleep each night. Over the next four weeks, try to go to bed at the same time every night and wake up at the same time every morning, aiming to get between seven and nine hours' sleep. Try to keep to this on the weekend as well as on week nights.

Record your goal bedtime, wake-up time, and total here:

Bedtime

Wake-up time

Total hours' sleep

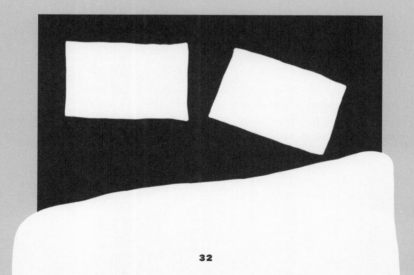

Form a bedtime ritual – your bedtime checklist

A circadian rhythm is the internal body clock cycle that tells you when to sleep, wake and eat. Your body clock can be affected by your environment, light and temperature, and some of the biggest culprits that affect our body clocks are smartphones, flatscreens and laptops. The blue light emitted from the screens can 'excite' your brain and deceive it into believing it is day instead of night, so you need to reduce your contact with blue light before bed.

Many foods and substances can also disturb the quality of sleep, so you should also watch your intake before bed. Stimulant effects and disrupted digestion can leave you restless all night and waking up groggy and unrested in the morning.

Start this ritual three hours before bedtime every night

- Set your phone to 'night mode', non-blue light, three hours before bedtime
- Stop using all electronics, including your phone and laptop, one hour before bed
- Avoid watching TV or films in bed
- Avoid heavy meals, nicotine, caffeine, sugar and carbonated drinks, alcohol and cannabis for at least three hours before bedtime.

 # Repeat your intention

Before you fall asleep in bed tonight, recite your statement of intent ten times in your mind, and feel the positive emotions associated with that intent. When you've affirmed your intentions, observe your hypnagogic state as long as you can before you slip into sleep. Tomorrow morning, observe your waking state.

You are four nights into your journey! Let your intentions continue to evolve and have vivid dreams tonight. See you tomorrow morning for day 5.

Sleeping Positions

Rise and shine, conscious dreamer! I hope that you had a delicious sleep in your improved dream surroundings. Today you're going to look at another practical aspect of sleeping: the positions in which you sleep.

☀ Record your waking and dreaming activity

Before you begin today's activities, record your dreams from last night in your dream journal. Note your bedtime, rising time and total sleeping time from last night, and record your wakening experience underneath your dream.

How do you sleep?

Do you sleep on your belly, back or side? Often it's only when you experience some kind of physical change or discomfort – back problems, neck injury, weight gain or pregnancy – that you begin to pay attention to the position you sleep in. Discomfort when you sleep in certain positions can affect the quality of your sleep and therefore your dreams.

Let's go over the six basic sleeping positions and find out which one works best for you right now.

The Freefaller

Sleeping on your stomach, sometimes called the prone position. Some people find this position is great to help ease snoring, but others find it causes neck and back pain. If you naturally sleep this way, try propping your forehead up on your pillow so your head and spine remain in a neutral position and you have room to breathe.

The Foetal Position

Sleeping on your side with your knees curled up toward your chest like a baby in its mother's womb. Some find this position causes hip pain; if that's the case for you, placing a pillow between your knees may help.

The Yearner

Sleeping on your side with your arms stretched out in front of you – as though you are yearning! If you don't always breathe easily while sleeping, this might be a good position to try out.

The Log

Just like the description, the sleeper in this stiff position lies on their side with their arms on either side of them. It's a position that can sometimes help the sleeper to stop snoring, but is one of the more uncomfortable positions for those who suffer from arthritis.

The Soldier

Also called the supine position, this can be a poor choice for snorers and those who experience low back pain, as it may prevent them from getting a restful night's sleep. However, there can be benefits to sleeping on your back, as you're less likely to experience neck pain. If you suffer from heartburn, try sleeping on your back with your head slightly elevated with a small pillow. Always avoid this position during pregnancy.

The Starfish

Often referred to as 'spread eagle', this position takes up a lot of room in the bed, so sharing sleeping time with a starfish sleeper can feel very cramped! Like everyone who sleeps on their back, starfish sleepers may be prone to snoring.

Draw an interpretational picture of your usual sleeping position below. Then, invent a new name for your sleeping position. It can be a silly or serious name. For example, 'The Banana'

Share a photo of your interpretive drawing and some words on how that sleeping position makes you feel.

Bedtime ritual

Begin going through the bedtime ritual from day 4, three hours before your ideal bedtime.

 Try out each sleep position on your bed

Allow 30 minutes of time to explore these positions before bedtime, spending five minutes in each of the six main sleep positions on your bed. While you are there trying out these positions, take some time to focus on your breath, recite your intention and hold the present moment as you soak up some quiet.

With each, ask yourself if the position feels intuitively natural. Then review the experiment and note the position you found most comfortable (it may not be the one you expected).

 Repeat your intention

Finally, when you're ready to go to sleep, settle into your favourite sleeping position, repeat your intention to yourself ten times, and observe your hypnagogic state as long as you can before you slip into sleep.

You are on your fifth night! Have a great sleep in your favoured sleeping position, let your intentions continue to evolve and have inspiring dreams tonight! See you tomorrow morning for day 6.

Dream Plants & Herbs

Good morning conscious dreamer! I hope that you are increasingly remembering and connecting with your dreams.

Today, you're going to look at using plants and herbs to help you dream more vividly and will be carrying out a dream tea ritual before bed. But first, please read through today's information carefully. If you decide not to use dream plants and herbs for health and safety reasons, or are not able to procure them today, don't worry: I have included some substitute drinks so that you can still partake in tonight's ritual.

 ## Record your waking and dreaming activity

Record your dreams from last night in your dream journal. Note your bedtime, rising time and total sleeping time from last night, and record your wakening experience underneath your dream. If you are still not able to remember any dreams from the past five nights, write down one you CAN remember, using the guidelines from day 2. Practise this whenever you struggle to remember a dream.

Oneirogens

There are a wide variety of herbs and plants out there that have long been associated with aiding sleep and dreaming. These herbs are called oneirogens from the Greek word oneiros (to dream) and gen (to create), and when made into a tea and consumed, can help trigger dreams and more restful sleep.

Working with these herbs and plants can improve your dream recall, trigger more dreams and assist you with any advanced dreamwork that you may be engaging in such as lucid, mutual or precognitive dreaming.

It's good to note that like all things, it's best to work with herbs in moderation. Refrain from going overboard, and when you are introducing new herbs into your life, you must always consider several factors: you need to be sure that you are not allergic to them before ingesting them, and you must **avoid ingesting dream herbs and plants if you are pregnant or have any health concerns**, unless approved by your health practitioner.

When introducing dream herbs and plants into your body, begin by introducing one herb at a time and paying attention to any reactions. If a reaction occurs, discontinue use immediately and consult a herbalist or healthcare professional.

Research and procure your herbs or plants

Your task for today is to research and procure some dream herbs and plants to aid your conscious dreaming practice. I recommend choosing from the list below, as all these herbs have been approved by the US Food and Drug Administrations, or are widely available to purchase as pre-mixed teas in supermarkets around the UK.

Here is a list of popular oneirogens that make perfect nightly dream teas:

Passion Flower

A very soft sedative that helps with vivid dreams.

Chamomile

Helps to soothe into sleep and aid calming dreams.
Warning: Chamomile has been known to cause allergies in people who are very sensitive to many allergens, but note this response is very rare.

Lemon Balm

A great little herb for soothing into sleep, improving mood and aiding in mental calmness. Lemon balm is considered a nootropic, meaning it helps improve cognitive performance!

Rosemary

Enhances dreaming and helps with dream memory recall.

Lavender

Boosts mood, calms the nerves and reduces stress for a better night's sleep.

 Share a photo of your dream plants or herbs and why you chose them.

Bedtime ritual

Begin going through the bedtime checklist from day 4, three hours before your ideal bedtime.

 # Dream tea ritual

If you feel safe and confident enough to incorporate dream herbs or plants into your conscious dreaming practice, a dream tea ritual before sleep can encourage more vivid dreaming.

If you have been unable to procure your dream herbs or plants, have any health concerns or are pregnant, you can still benefit from the calming effects of this ritual by substituting dream tea with a safe caffeine-free hot drink, a glass of warm lemon water or simply a cup of water.

Ritual steps:

- Prepare your herb in a cup or teapot and add boiling water
- Let the herb steep for ten minutes
- Add honey or agave syrup as desired
- Sit in quiet meditative reflection
- With mindful intent for dreaming, drink your dream tea
- Settle into bed, keeping your intention from day 1 in mind.

☾ Repeat your intention

Finally, when you're ready to go to sleep, settle into your favourite sleeping position, repeat your intention to yourself ten times and observe your hypnagogic state as long as you can before you slip into sleep.

You are on your sixth night – you've spent almost a week as a conscious dreamer! See you tomorrow morning for day 7.

Meditation

Good morning!
    I hope that you had some active dreaming last night and began to explore your dream world. Today you're going to learn how to improve, prepare and deepen your dream space with meditation.

☀ Record your waking and dreaming activity

But first, record your dreams from last night in your dream journal. Note your bedtime, rising time and total sleeping time from last night, and your wakening experience.
    If you drank dream tea last night, do you feel it made for different dreaming experiences? Note your observations in your journal.

What happens to your mind when you meditate?

The more mindful and aware you are in your waking life, the more chance you have of becoming aware within the dream state. It can also relieve stress and anxiety, promote emotional health, reduce memory loss, help to lengthen your attention span, and improve sleep.

Meditation trains your mind to focus and redirect your thoughts at will. You don't need to be a spiritual guru in order to do it. You can practise small exercises every day to help increase your awareness of yourself and your surroundings.

A good start to understanding the benefits of meditation on your dreaming practice is to understand what goes on biologically in our brains when we meditate, as it can be quite similar to what happens when we sleep.

When we fall asleep and travel through the different sleep stages, our brainwaves fluctuate. Brainwaves are the electrical impulses triggered in the brain when billions of neurons communicate with each other. Some brainwaves are fast and some are slow. I like to visualize brainwaves as water waves: the slowest are like deep currents under the ocean, while the fastest are choppy like a rapid flowing river. We experience faster brainwaves when we are engaged with everyday tasks, and slower ones when we are relaxing in more creative and dreamlike states.

Our brainwaves speed up when we are dreaming, but when we reach the deepest stage in our sleep cycle – stage four – our brainwaves are at their slowest. We can recreate and access these slower dreamlike states in our waking life – slowing down our brainwaves – by practising meditation, daydreaming and hypnosis. This will not only help you relax, reduce overthinking and anxiety, and improve your awareness of the present moment, but will help strengthen your control over your mind. All of these things will help you become more aware of and lucid in your dreams in the long run.

Use your daydreams to meditate

You can slow down brainwaves and induce a more meditative state of mind with this quirky daytime meditation!

Set aside ten minutes to sit still in quiet meditation and observe the daydreams that unfold in your mind's eye. This is best carried out a few hours after caffeine! Just let your mind wander. If you notice your mind returning to any worries or undone tasks, repeat this affirmation:

'I give myself permission to use this time

to relax, and forget about my worries.

There is nothing that cannot wait.'

As you are daydreaming, doodle in the space here. By the end of this exercise, your mind should have slowed down, and you should feel more relaxed and grounded.

 Share a photo of your doodling and some words about your daydream meditation.

Bedtime and dream tea ritual

Begin going through your bedtime checklist from day 4, three hours before your ideal bedtime. Prepare your dream tea to take to bed with you.

Slow your brainwaves before bed

Now let's practise slowing down your brainwaves with this nighttime meditation exercise! You will need technology for this activity, so make sure that you do not carry it out less than one hour before your bedtime.

When you are ready to begin, find some binaural beats or isotopic tones online. When you've found something you like, plug in your headphones or play it out loud. Set aside 15 minutes to sit in quiet meditation, and focus your awareness on the tone coming through your headphones, or surrounding you.

After your meditation, spend a few minutes recording the details of your experience in your dream journal.

🌙 Repeat your intention

Finally, when you're ready to go to sleep, repeat your intention to yourself ten times, and observe your hypnagogic state as long as you can before you slip into sleep. Tomorrow morning observe your state upon awakening.

You've completed your first week! Have a productive time surfing through your dreams tonight. See you tomorrow morning for day 8.

PART II:
Dreaming

Dream Recall

Good morning dreamer! Welcome to part two of your journey, where you are going to be focusing on enhancing your awareness within your dream space, and learning how you can better interact with your dreams.

Dreams are the blueprint to your unconscious mind: they are full of insight, guidance, mystery and inspiration! For the next week, you will be traversing through your dreams in order to map out the framework of your unconscious zones. Think of your dreams as a vast ocean. You are on a boat within this immense watery landscape with no map. As you travel through the great waters you see various things: a tropical island, a giant squid, a mermaid floating on a giant shell and tiger in a hot air balloon. As you come across these landmarks, draw them on your map. That way you become familiar with the terrain should you need to journey through it again.

First and foremost, you need to be able remember these experiences so that you can record them, and connect the dots between your dreams. Many dreamers struggle to recall their dreams at night, so today you will be trying out some activities to improve your dream recall skills.

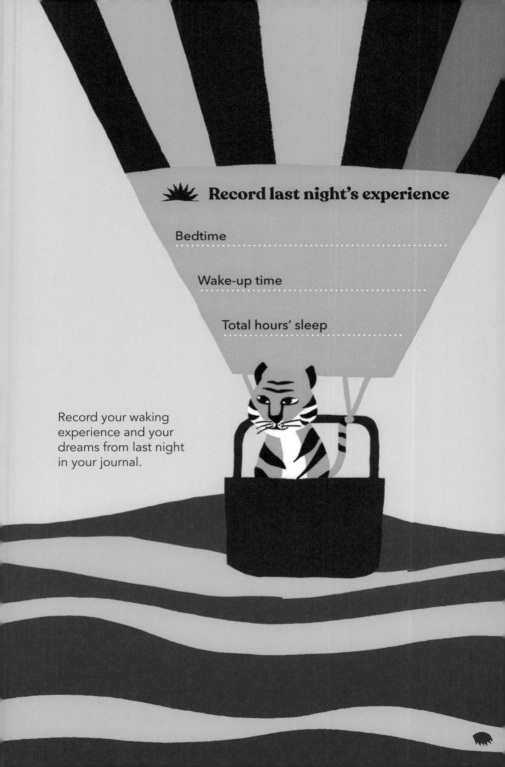

Record last night's experience

Bedtime ....

Wake-up time ....

Total hours' sleep ....

Record your waking
experience and your
dreams from last night
in your journal.

 Create memory prompts

- Tell yourself throughout the day that you will remember your dreams. Write down 'I will remember my dreams tonight' ten times on a piece of paper every hour. Set yourself an alarm on your phone or make a note on a piece of paper to remind you.
- Make a note, drawing or poster that says, 'What was I just dreaming?' and put it somewhere that will catch your eye when you wake up.
- Choose an object that you can begin to use as a prompt for remembering your dreams. It could be an unusual object, a special heirloom, or something silly and fun. Put this object near to your bed, and look to it when you need help remembering your dreams. You will quickly begin to associate this object with better dream recall.
- Create some colourful flashcards using paper, scissors and pens. Look through your recent dreams and choose some visual elements that you can use as content for your flashcards. Write down or draw a visual element from your dream on each card. For example, if you had a dream about a fish that was swimming in the sky, with the sun and clouds close to a snow-capped mountain, you could create the following flashcards: fish, sun, clouds, snow-capped mountain. Once you've made your cards, pick out a random card a few times during the day to see if it triggers you to remember extra details about the dream.

 Share a photo of your flashcards.

Bedtime and dream tea ritual

Begin the bedtime checklist from day 4, three hours before bedtime. Prepare your dream tea to take to bed with you.

 ## Prepare to recall

Read through your dream journal before you go to sleep tonight to help your dream memory recall, and trigger new dreams.

Write in your dream journal 'I will remember my dreams tonight' ten times before you fall asleep.

 ## Repeat your intention

As you fall asleep, repeat your intention to yourself ten times, observing your hypnagogic state as long as you can. Tomorrow morning, do not rush yourself getting out of bed. Try to stay within the zone of your dreams and let your dreams replay in your mind.

Have vivid dreams tonight, and see you tomorrow morning for day 9.

Reality Checks & Lucid Dreams

Good morning conscious dreamer! I hope you had meaningful dreams last night and that your dream memory recall is improving. Today we are going to take your dream training up a notch and focus on techniques and activities to help you lucid dream.

Record your waking and dreaming activity

Before you begin today's activities, record your dreams from last night in your dream journal. Note your bedtime, rising time and total sleeping time from last night, and record your wakening experience.

If you are struggling to remember your dreams, look to your dream object to help trigger recall.

What is a lucid dream?

Lucid dreaming is a phenomena where you become aware that you are in a dream while you are sleeping. Lucid dreaming is not only the ability to know that you are in a dream, but the ability to control what happens in it, too.

Here's an example of a lucid dream: you are walking down the street when you see a gigantic rhino cross the road. You ask yourself where it came from, while locking eyes with the animal as it approaches you. You go into fight or flight mode, and your panic alerts you to the fact that you are in a dream and there is no danger. The rhino charges into you but you are not afraid, and you open your arms as it transforms into your friend, who you hug.

Lucid dreaming can be very transformative. It is a profound and vivid experience and you will never forget your first lucid dream. When we realize that we have the ability to become conscious in dreams and to control or create things within them, we can begin to question our perception of reality and the world that exists around us.

And teaching yourself to notice and get into the habit of questioning reality is one of the most important foundations to becoming a lucid dreamer.

Reality Checks

A reality check is a moment when you question your perception of reality. Reality checks are one of the best activities for triggering lucid dreams, but are something that we need to train ourselves to do. Performing a reality check requires a total shift of your awareness and complete focus on the task at hand. You must become completely absorbed in what you are doing.

Doing a minimum of eight reality checks per day will help you develop a great habit, and training your mind to question reality while you are awake will train your mind to question reality while you are dreaming.

Today, you are going to carry out one reality check per hour for a total of eight hours. Make sure you keep this book on you to refer back to each hour. There are eight different types below, and you should perform a different one each hour. Tick off each reality check once you have done it, and aim to get into the habit of doing these every day from now onwards.

Each time you perform a reality check, ask yourself these three questions: *Am I dreaming? Is this reality? Am I awake?*

Reality check 1:
check your memo

Create a drawing or poster that says 'Am I dreaming?' and put it somewhere that will trigger you to do a reality check.

Reality check 2:
check your reflection

Look in the mirror and study your reflection. Ask yourself if your face looks normal. Often in dreams, your reflection in the mirror will begin to morph and distort.

Reality check 3:
check your hands

Try to push a finger through your palm. If you are dreaming, you might find that you are able to push your finger through the palm of your hand.

Reality check 4:
check solid objects

Push your hand against a solid object and hold it there for 30 seconds. When dreaming, you may be able to push your hand through solid-looking objects.

Reality check 5: check the time

Pay attention to clocks, the time on your phone, laptop or any other time-keeping device. When we look at a clock in a dream, the time may jump all over the place.

Reality check 6: check your breath

Pinch your nose and close your mouth. Can you still breathe? If you are dreaming, you might still be able to breathe with your mouth closed and your nose pinched.

Reality check 7: check the sky

Look up at the sky, the clouds and the colours of the sun. Does all appear normal? If you are dreaming, the sky might begin to dramatically change, objects might appear or the weather might become strange.

Reality check 8: check a marking

Choose a marking on your body such as a birthmark, scar or tattoo. Analyze its texture, colour and form and ask yourself if it appears normal. In dreams, your mark might begin to morph, or look distorted or different in some way.

 Share a photo of your 'Am I dreaming?' drawing or poster in your chosen setting.

Bedtime and dream tea ritual

Begin to go through the bedtime checklist from day 4, three hours before bedtime. Prepare your dream tea to take to bed with you.

Repeat your intention

As you fall asleep, repeat your intention to yourself ten times, observing your hypnagogic state as long as you can.

Well done conscious dreamer. See you tomorrow morning for day 10.

W.I.L.D. Meditation

Rise and shine, conscious dreamer! I hope last night's dream adventures were profound for you.

You have been observing your hypnagogic state as you fall asleep for a week now, and today, you are going to be observing it during the daytime using a lucid dreaming technique called W.I.L.D. meditation. The benefit of observing your hypnagogic state during the day is that your body will be less fatigued, allowing you to observe more without falling into sleep.

 ## Record your waking and dreaming activity

Record your dreams from last night in your dream journal. Note your bedtime, rising time and total sleeping time from last night, and record your wakening experience.

 ## Keep practising your reality checks

Commit to performing one reality check per hour today for eight hours. Perform each of the eight reality checks from day 9. Set yourself a recurring reminder on your phone, or leave yourself a note somewhere you will see.

Wake Induced Lucid Dreaming

Wake Induced Lucid Dreaming (W.I.L.D. meditation) is the ability to enter into a lucid dream from your waking state. Your mind stays totally conscious as your body goes to sleep. Part of mastering Wake Induced Lucid Dreaming is learning how to train your mind to observe and be present with the dream-like images that evolve in your mind when your eyes are closed. W.I.L.D. meditation can help you become more present, aware and observant within your dreamstates, and when you become advanced at it, you might be able to go straight into a lucid dream.

Take a walk on the W.I.L.D. side

In this exercise, you will be attempting to keep your mind focused, observant and conscious as your body falls asleep. The aim of this exercise is to remain conscious or 'lucid' as you begin to see the dream imagery unfold in your mind.

Set aside 20 minutes today for your W.I.L.D. meditation practice. It is best to carry out this activity at home or in a comfortable place where you can relax and lie quietly without being disturbed.

Try to memorize as many of the steps below as you can before you begin. This exercise takes time and patience to perfect, so don't be discouraged if you don't manage it the first time around and need to refer back to the book.

When you are ready to begin:

- Set a timer for 20 minutes
- Lie down comfortably on your back and relax your body
- Close your eyes
- Focus on breathing slowly in through your nose and out through your mouth
- Try to detach yourself from any niggling thoughts or emotions that crop up and deeply relax
- Observe imagery, shapes, colours and sounds that come to mind
- Allow your mind and imagination to wander and create what will become your dream scene
- Repeat to yourself 'I'm going into a dream'
- As the dream scene imagery unfolds, become active in it, letting your imagination lead the way without questioning the details
- Allow yourself to play in your dream scene, resisting the temptation to fall asleep, until your timer goes off.

Paint the scene

Draw the scene you created during your W.I.L.D. meditation. Perhaps a jungle scene with tropical plants, vines and planets from far-off galaxies.

 Share a photo of your drawing of your W.I.L.D. meditation.

 ## Bedtime and dream tea ritual

Begin the bedtime checklist from day 4, three hours before bedtime. Prepare your dream tea to take to bed with you.

 ## Repeat your intention

As you fall asleep, repeat your intention to yourself ten times and feel the positive emotions associated with that intent.

🌙 Revisit your dream scene

Observe your hypnagogic state as long as you can. See if
you can revisit the scene you created during your W.I.L.D.
meditation earlier today before you slip into sleep to see if
it triggers any lucid dreaming.

See you tomorrow morning for day 11.

Dream Signs

Good morning, conscious dreamer! Have you experienced your first lucid dream yet? Don't worry if you haven't; practice and patience is the key.

Today, you will be exploring dream signs and learning how to spot them. Dream signs are visual triggers that are unique to you. Once you train yourself to spot them, they can help you become lucid within a dream, so you'll want to pay close attention today!

 ## Record your waking and dreaming activity

Record your dreams from last night in your dream journal. Note your bedtime, rising time and total sleeping time from last night, and record your wakening experience.

 ## Schedule your reality checks and W.I.L.D. meditation

Set yourself a timer or alarm that goes off once per hour for eight hours. Perform each of the reality checks from day 9, and set aside 20 minutes today to practise your W.I.L.D. meditation.

What is a dream sign?

A dream sign is a prompt, hint or clue that, when recognized, can indicate that you are in a dream. Dream signs come in wide variety of shapes, scenes and imagery, and will be recurring. Training yourself to notice them while you are dreaming can help you to become lucid.

Dream signs can be objects and symbols, places such as your childhood home, and people such as loved ones (we often see the same people in our dreams time and time again). While your dream signs will be unique to you, common signs include cars, boats, trees, clocks, birds, water, houses, windows, mirrors, the moon, and staircases.

Once you have identified your dream signs, you can begin to use them to perform reality checks. For example, a dream sign of mine is a symbol of an eye. When I was a teenager, I would draw them so much that I began to dream about them. This symbol became one of my dream signs, and now, I can use it to perform reality checks, and trigger myself to become lucid while dreaming. Now, whenever I see an eye symbol in my waking or dreaming life, I ask myself these questions:

Am I dreaming? Is this reality? Am I awake?

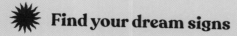 **Find your dream signs**

For this activity, you will begin to identify some of your dream signs. You will need your dream journal for this. Read through all of the dreams you have documented since the start of this journey. Can you spot anything interesting? Record everything you find from each of the categories below in the space provided. If something recurs, you can make a tally mark next to it each time it crops up.

Objects

....

....

Animals

....

....

Insects

....

....

People

....

....

Places

....

....

Numbers

....

....

Symbols

....

....

Music

....

....

Food

....

....

Nature

....

....

Colours

....

....

Aromas

....

....

Other

....

....

....

Did you notice many recurring features in your dreams?
    If you struggled to find any recurring symbols or patterns
at this stage of your journey, don't worry! Just note down
anything interesting. You can revisit this list in the future to
see if anything has begun to recur since.

Create a dream sign

As well as identifying and observing them, you can also consciously create your own dream signs, like I did with the symbol of an eye. Draw a symbol that you would like to become a dream symbol on a piece of paper and repeat it a few times. Make sure that it's something you can replicate, and continue to doodle this symbol as you go about your day. You'll want to get into the habit of seeing and drawing this symbol frequently from now on.

Share a photo of the dream symbol you've created.

 ## Bedtime and dream tea ritual

Begin to go through the bedtime checklist three hours before bedtime. Prepare your dream tea to take to bed with you.

 ## Draw your dream symbol

Draw your dream symbol ten times on a piece of paper just before your bedtime. Take your time and don't rush as you focus on the task.

 ## Repeat your intention

As you fall asleep, repeat your intention to yourself ten times and visualize your dream symbol. Observe your hypnagogic state as long as you can.

I hope you find your dream symbol in your dreams tonight. See you tomorrow morning for day 12.

DAY 12

Dream Germination

Good morning conscious dreamer! I hope that you are starting to find a good groove in your practice, and that you are continuing with your morning and bedtime activities every day. These repeated exercises are the most important part of your practice, so keep up the good work.

Today you will be learning about the technique of dream germination. It's going to be a busy day!

 ## Record your waking and dreaming activity

Record your dreams from last night in your dream journal, your bedtime, rising time and total sleeping time from last night, and record your wakening experience.

 ## Switch up your reality checks

Set yourself a timer or alarm that goes off once per hour for eight hours. Each time it goes off, draw the dream sign that you created yesterday ten times on a piece of paper, and ask yourself: *Am I dreaming? Is this reality? Am I awake?*

What does it mean to germinate a dream?

Dream germination, or dream incubation, is the technique of planting an idea in your mind in order to cause yourself to dream about a certain topic or scenario. This is a very helpful technique if you want to use your dreams to problem solve or find creative inspiration.

Germinating a dream is similar to germinating a plant seed. Like a plant starts with a seed, a dream starts with an idea. When you plant an idea or 'seed' in your mind, you can encourage a certain dream to grow.

 ## Create a moodboard

Before you begin to incubate a dream, it's important to determine what you want to get out of it. Do you want to create something or solve a problem? Ask yourself what your goal is, and revisit the intention you set yourself at the beginning of this book for guidance.

Create a mindmap or moodboard as you develop your goal, and begin to think about the surroundings, characters, scenarios and objects that could feature in your dream. You can draw images, print photos off from online or create a photo album on your phone or laptop.

 Share a photo of your moodboard or mindmap.

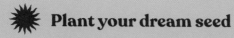 Plant your dream seed

Once you have an idea of what you want to achieve from your dream, you can begin to work on the details.

Select your seed

Write what you want to do in or get out of your dream here. For example, 'I want to fly in my dreams and feel free.'

....

....

....

....

....

....

....

....

....

....

....

....

....

....

Bedtime and dream tea ritual

Begin to go through your bedtime checklist (see page 33) three hours before bedtime.

 Revisit your dream scene

When you get into bed, focus your mind on revisiting the scene you began to germinate during your W.I.L.D. meditation today, observing your hypnagogic state as long as you can as you slip into sleep.

See you tomorrow morning for day 13.

Wake Back To Bed Technique

Rise and shine conscious dreamer! Did you manage to step into the dream you began to germinate yesterday?

Today will be a quieter day for activities, as you will need all your energy to practise the wake back to bed technique later. Rest up today, as this technique will require you to wake up early tomorrow.

Record your waking and dreaming activity

Record your dreams from last night in your dream journal. Don't forget, if you're still struggling to recall your dreams, you can look to your dream object for help. Note your bedtime, rising time and total sleeping time from last night, and record your wakening experience.

Reality checks

Schedule eight reality checks for today. For each check, draw your dream sign ten times on a piece of paper and ask yourself: *Am I dreaming? Is this reality? Am I awake?*

 Share a photo of your dream sign drawings and reflect on how your reality checks are going.

Wake Back to Bed Technique

The wake back to bed technique is the practice of interrupting your sleep cycle in order to increase your chances of achieving lucidity in your dreams.

The technique interrupts your sleep cycle at the REM stage: the time when your brain is most active and you experience your dreams. Waking yourself up during the REM phase can increase your chances of lucid dreaming.

When used occasionally, this technique can help you enter straight into a lucid dream. However, it is important not to practise this technique more than once every week, as you will disrupt your natural body clock and sleep rhythm. Tip: a great time to practise is once on the weekend.

If you're embracing all the other practices outlined in your journey through this book, you won't need to alter your sleep cycle regularly to induce lucid or vivid dreaming. But this technique is still fun and safe to use as an occasional experiment.

Bedtime and dream tea ritual

Begin to go through your bedtime checklist three hours before bedtime.

When you look at your phone or alarm clock for the last time, set an additional alarm to go off two hours before your usual one.

Drink your dream tea shortly before bed, and read through the next activity just before you settle down for the night. Try to visualize yourself waking up and doing these exercises as you drift into sleep.

When your first alarm goes off, turn it off and go through the steps below.

Wake back to bed

1 Lie back in bed.

2 Let your mind wake up by counting back from 20 and let your body remain still and relaxed.

3 Begin to engage in W.I.L.D. meditation, immersing yourself in the dream scene that you began to germinate yesterday as you drift back into sleep. You may be able to move straight into a lucid dream.

Good luck with your wake back to bed experiment tonight and see you tomorrow morning for day 14.

Mutual Dreaming

Good morning conscious dreamer. I hope last night's wake back to bed experiment helped you to better connect with your dreams! Today you will be exploring the exciting possibilities of mutual dreaming.

Record your waking and dreaming activity

Record your dreams from last night in your dream journal, your bedtime, rising time and total sleeping time from last night, and your wakening experience. Reflect on your experience using the wake back to bed technique. Did it work?

 ## Reality checks

Schedule eight reality checks of your choice for today, but make sure that you use the dream sign reality check from yesterday for at least one of them.

What is mutual dreaming?

Mutual dreaming is when two or more people share the same dream or have a dream that shares very similar scenes or symbols. Mutual dreamers will also sometimes appear in each other's shared dreams.

Although the concept of mutual dreaming contradicts the laws of modern science, many people report experiencing this phenomenon, especially with family members or friends.

There are many theories that support or debunk mutual dreaming. Some put the phenomenon down to uncanny coincidences and hoaxes, while some more complex theories view mutual dreaming as a type of interconnectivity that taps into the collective unconscious, a form of telepathy, or some sort of quantum entanglement.

But wherever you stand with your thoughts on mutual dreaming, it is still a great technique to explore and experiment with.

Plan your mutual dreaming experiment

Mutual dreams can be planned in advance, so find yourself a fellow dreamer who is up for the experiment.

- Record the name of your fellow dreamer here:

....

- With your partner, set a joint intention to appear in each other's dreams tonight. Write down 'I am going to find [the name of your fellow dreamer] in my dreams tonight' on a piece of paper and ask your partner to do the same. Hang on to this piece of paper.

- Next, plan the dream scene that you would like to meet each other in. For example, you could visualize opening a door to a place you are both familiar with, and finding your fellow dreamer there waiting to greet you on the other side.

- Record the dream scene that you would like to share with your partner on the pieces of paper with your shared intention on.

- When your dream is planned, keep hold of your piece of paper and save it for tonight's activity.

 Expand your dreaming circle and post a selfie or drawing with the caption 'Mutual Dreamer'. Use the hashtag #consciousdreamer to find other dreamers on the same journey, and send them a supportive message if you wish.

Bedtime and dream tea ritual

Begin the bedtime checklist three hours before bedtime.
Prepare your dream tea to take to bed with you.

Connect with your fellow dreamer

When you are ready to fall asleep, find your piece of paper
from earlier and read through it five times. Turn off the
lights and as you fall asleep, repeat your mutual dreaming
intention to yourself, and visualize connecting with your
friend in your mutual dream scene.

Well done today and good luck with your experiment!
See you tomorrow morning for day 15.

PART III:
Waking

Dream Genres

Good morning conscious dreamer! How did last night's mutual dreaming experiment go? Welcome to part three of your journey, where we will be focusing on what you can do when you wake up to connect with your dreams even further.

Today we are going to dive into unpacking and understanding dream categories (genres). But first, complete your regular morning activities below.

 ## Record last night's experience

Record your dreams from last night in your dream journal, your bedtime, rising time and total sleeping time from last night, and your wakening experience. Then reflect on your mutual dreaming experiment. Did you run into your dreaming partner? At some point today, compare your dream with your friend's to see if there were any similarities.

 ## Reality checks

Schedule eight reality checks of your choice for today. Draw the dream symbol you created ten times for one of your checks, while asking yourself your reality check questions.

Dream categories

As a conscious dreamer, it's really helpful to get organized with your dream journal. Part of this organization is slotting your dreams into categories. This can help you begin to decode and analyze your dreams more efficiently.

Dreams are like mini films with moving images, narratives, plot lines and moods. Applying the same category system from films to your dreams can make your dream journalling process more fun, and it helps you to see the emotions attached to your dreams.

The most important aspect of categorizing your dream is to determine what the predominant emotion was. Your emotions are all clues as to which category to choose. For example:

EMOTION	GENRE
Excited	*Action/Adventure*
Love	*Romance*
Fear	*Horror*
Confused	*Mystery/Surreal*
Amused	*Comedy*
Profound/Mystical	*Fantasy*

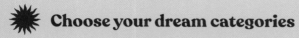

Choose your dream categories

Go through your dream journal and write down the category that you feel applies to each dream. Write the category next to the dream.

Title your dreams

Just as film directors name their films, come up with a title for your dreams. Naming your dream will help to give it a meaning personal to you. It will also help to give it meaning and aid you in incorporating the advice it is trying to give you into your waking life.

To spark your inspiration when titling your dreams, consider the following questions:

- Was there a story or theme?
- Were there any special characters or objects?
- Was there a particular image that stood out?

An example: I had a dream that I was sitting in a big tree and below me a pig was running back and forth in the grass. I jumped out of the tree to have a closer look at the pig. The pig turned into a boy. Then I saw a white rabbit hopping past. I chased the rabbit and it jumped into a rubbish bin.

- Story or theme: chasing or the act of chasing something
- Special characters: a pig, a boy and a white rabbit
- Images: big tree, green grass, rubbish bin.

An example dream title: The Adventures of Chasing Pig Boy and the Disappearing Rabbit.

Go through your dream journal and create some dream titles for the dreams you've recorded throughout your journey. Add the title next to the date of your dream.

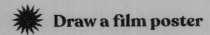 # Draw a film poster

Draw a poster below for one of your dreams as if it was being released as a film.

 Share your film dream poster and a short blurb about your 'film'.

Bedtime and dream tea ritual

Begin the bedtime checklist from day 4, three hours before bedtime. Prepare your dream tea to take to bed with you.

 ## Revisit your intention

As you close day 15, check in with the intention you set yourself at the beginning of this book. Take a piece of paper to bed with you tonight and reflect on how you are progressing with your intention.

As you fall asleep, repeat your intention to yourself ten times, observing your hypnagogic state as long as you can.

Great job today! You are officially halfway through your journey. See you tomorrow morning for day 16.

Precognitive Dreaming

Good morning conscious dreamer! I hope your nightly dreams are becoming more connected.

Today we are going to explore precognitive dreaming, sometimes referred to as future vision or psychic dreaming. Most of us can recount a time when we experienced some kind of foreshadowing in our lives, whether it was in a dream or in our waking lives. Whether you believe in these experiences or not, these events can make us question the nature of our reality, and that's not necessarily a bad thing! A true conscious dreamer gets into that mode on a regular basis, so let's explore.

Record your waking and dreaming activity

Record your dreams from last night in your dream journal, your bedtime, rising time and total sleeping time from last night, and your wakening experience.

Schedule your reality checks and W.I.L.D. meditation

Schedule eight reality checks for today, including your dream symbol check. If there's one check you find particularly effective, you might like to start practising it a few times a day.

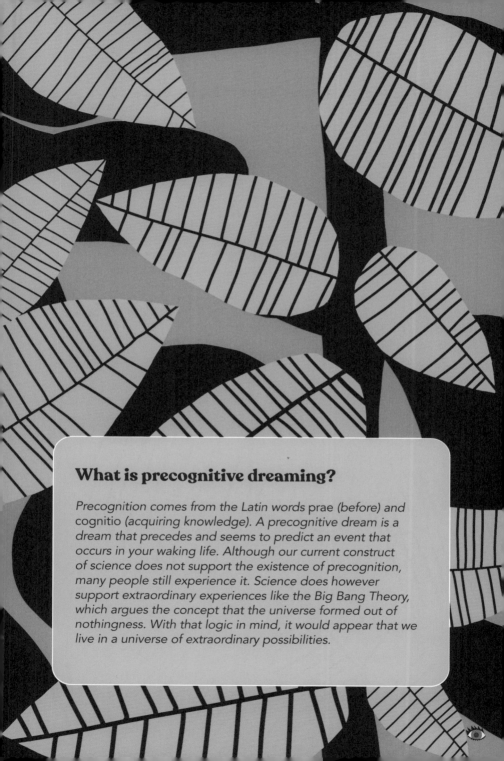

What is precognitive dreaming?

Precognition comes from the Latin words prae (before) and cognitio (acquiring knowledge). A precognitive dream is a dream that precedes and seems to predict an event that occurs in your waking life. Although our current construct of science does not support the existence of precognition, many people still experience it. Science does however support extraordinary experiences like the Big Bang Theory, which argues the concept that the universe formed out of nothingness. With that logic in mind, it would appear that we live in a universe of extraordinary possibilities.

Look to the past to see the future!

Your dream journal will serve as a proof of record for any precognitive dreams that you experience. When an event occurs in your waking life, you can go back to the dated dream in your journal and confirm that it was in fact correct. Your dreams can predict the very mundane as well as the extraordinary. For example, you dream about a pink and black plant, and the next day, somebody gifts you a similar plant.

Go back through your dream journal and read your dreams. Pay attention to any dreams that may hold clues to events that have since occurred in your waking life. If you aren't able to spot any just yet, don't worry! Just be sure to look out for examples of precognitive dreaming in the future when you reflect on your dream journal, and bear it in mind as you observe events in your waking life.

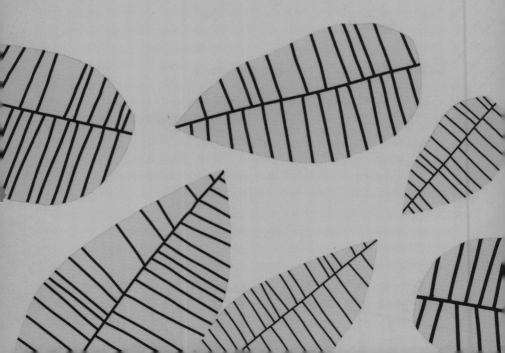

Bedtime and dream tea ritual

Begin the bedtime checklist from day 4, three hours before bedtime. Prepare your dream tea to take to bed with you.

Revisit the dream you are germinating

As you fall asleep, imagine yourself in the dream scene you are trying to germinate, observing your hypnagogic state as long as you can, and potentially stepping straight into it.

Great work! You have accomplished day 16 of your journey. I hope your dreams are symbolic and intriguing. See you tomorrow morning for day 17.

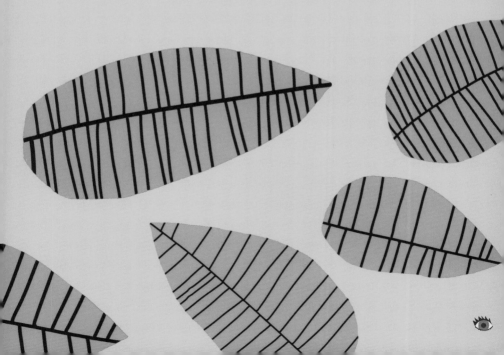

Decoding Your Dreams

Rise and shine, conscious dreamer! I hope last night's dream adventures brought you a sense of wonder.

Today you are going to learn how to begin decoding your dreams. You will have begun to analyze your dreams already for previous activities, but today you will be focusing more intently on understanding and listening to what they are telling you.

Dreams are the blueprint of your unconscious mind, and as your dreams are uniquely tailored for you, by you, you are the perfect person to decode their mystery. You have all the answers inside of you, but unlocking the answers can take a bit of mindfulness, reflection, contemplation and detective work.

Record your waking and dreaming activity

Record your dreams from last night in your dream journal, your bedtime, rising time and total sleeping time from last night, and your wakening experience.

 ## Schedule your reality checks and W.I.L.D. meditation

Schedule eight reality checks for today, including your dream symbol check.

Set aside 20 minutes to practise your W.I.L.D. meditation. You can focus on the dream you are germinating, or explore a completely new scene. Take this time today to get creative and have fun!

Decode your dream symbols

Now that you have had some time since day 11 to notice any more recurring dream symbols, it's time to reflect on their meaning. This process of decoding can be fun and very insightful.

1 Write down five of your recurring dream signs or symbols on a piece of paper. Next to them, write the first thing that comes to mind when you consider what each symbol might represent. For example, a white rabbit represents magic and mystery.

2 Once you've done this, search online or in a dream dictionary for the meaning of your dream symbols. A symbol may have multiple interpretations and one might particularly resonate with you. Write down what your research tells you each symbol means.

3 Finally, record once again what you think your dream symbols mean now that you've had time to explore their potential meanings, noting what your personal dream symbols mean in the greater context of your life. Are they telling you that you need something, or that you need to make some changes? Listen to your gut and intuition – the ultimate meaning of each symbol will come from within you. For example, I see that a white rabbit appearing in my dreams is a sign that I need to welcome more mystery and magic into my life.

 Get creative

Make a collage of your personal dream symbols and place it in your bedroom, where they can act as a reminder of what your dreams are suggesting you need.

 Share a photo of your dream symbol collage.

Bedtime and dream tea ritual

Begin the bedtime checklist from day 4, three hours before bedtime. Prepare your dream tea to take to bed with you.

 ## Revisit your intention

As you fall asleep, repeat your intention to yourself ten times, observing your hypnagogic state as long as you can.

See you tomorrow morning for day 18.

Dream Maps

Morning conscious dreamer! I hope you are ready to continue delving more deeply into the meaning of your dreams.

Today, you are going to be exploring your dream locations and attempting to return to one in particular. This can get very exciting and exploratory as a conscious dreamer.

But first, carry out your usual morning checks.

 ## Record your waking and dreaming activity

Record your dreams from last night in your dream journal, your bedtime, rising time and total sleeping time from last night, and your wakening experience.

 ## Schedule your reality checks

Schedule eight reality checks for today, including your dream symbol check.

Locating your dreams

The places you visit in your dreams are deeply symbolic and hold big clues, but often we don't pay attention to this aspect of dreaming.

Read through your dream journal and think back to any notable dreams in your past. Are there any particular places that you visit frequently in your dreams, or locations that stand out? Jot down a brief description of five dream locations on a large piece of paper and give each location a name.

For example, when I dream about the white rabbit, I dream about a park near my childhood home where there is green grass and a big tree. I call this area Green Acres.

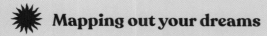 # Mapping out your dreams

Now it's time to make a map! Naming and mapping your dream locations can help to bridge the gap between your dream world and waking reality. Creating a map will also help you go back to certain locations in your dreams, and you may even be able to become lucid when you spot the locations from your map in your dreams.

For this activity, you will need:

The other side of your large piece of paper
Coloured pens and pencils
A laptop and printer (optional)
Tape or glue (optional)

Before you begin drawing or sticking images of your dream locations on your piece of paper, sit quietly and let your intuition guide you as to where on the paper your locations should go. Go with your gut instinct! For example, for me, Green Acres feels like it's located up to the left of my map.

Draw as many dream locations as you can. There might be recurring locations from dreams as well as those that you dreamt of when you were a child. Some might feel lovely and beautiful, others scary, dreadful or even boring!

When you are finished, put your map up on your wall next to your bed to serve as a reminder and blueprint for all of the locations you adventure through in your dream worlds.

 Share a photo of your dream map.

 ## Bedtime and dream tea ritual

Begin the bedtime checklist from day 4, three hours before bedtime. Prepare your dream tea to take to bed with you.

 ## W.I.L.D. meditation

Schedule 20 minutes just before your bedtime to practise your W.I.L.D. meditation. When you are settled in bed, look at your dream map and choose one of your locations to venture to in your dreams tonight. Use this setting as the focus for your W.I.L.D. meditation, and allow yourself to explore it as you drift off to sleep. You may be able to step straight into a lucid dream!

Goodnight, and see you tomorrow morning for day 19.

DAY 19

Daydreaming

Good morning, conscious dreamer! I hope you managed to visit somewhere fantastic in your dreams last night.

Throughout your journey, you've been focusing on the dreams you have when you sleep. Today, you are going to be exploring the dreams you have when you're awake: your daydreams! You will need to keep your dream journal with you as you go about your day today.

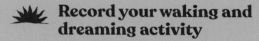 ## Record your waking and dreaming activity

Record your dreams from last night in your dream journal, your bedtime, rising time and total sleeping time from last night, and your wakening experience.

 ## Schedule your reality checks

Schedule eight reality checks for today, including your dream symbol check.

Follow your daydreams

Daydreams are a powerful way of brainstorming new ideas, setting intentions and planting the seeds for manifesting new things in your life.

Set aside time today to encourage your mind to follow eight daydreams. If your schedule and surroundings allow it, you might like to carry out the next exercise following each of your reality checks.

You are going to be recording eight daydreams in your dream journal. After performing each of your reality checks, go through the following steps:

- Sit in quiet reflection for five minutes
- Let your mind come to stillness
- Observe what comes into your mind
- Allow the scene to unfold and your mind to wander
- Watch your daydream in a detached way, as if you are watching a film
- After five minutes, write down what happened in your daydream and how it made you feel. Note where you were, who else was there, what you were doing, and any sensory experiences that were prominent such as colour, smells or sounds.

For example, I watch a raindrop land on
a leaf, where it transforms into a butterfly,
and then soars up into the sky and
becomes a firework.

Draw the colour palette for your daydreams

As you record each daydream, create a colour palette for each one in the space below. Colour is something we don't always pay attention to in our dreams, and you might be surprised at how consistent or varied in colour your dreams are.

 Share a photo of your colour palette, and if you're comfortable to, some details of a daydream.

 ## Bedtime and dream tea ritual

Begin the bedtime checklist from day 4, three hours before bedtime. Prepare your dream tea to take to bed with you.

 ## Continue your daydream during your W.I.L.D. meditation

Lie down comfortably 20 minutes before your bedtime, and prepare to engage in W.I.L.D. meditation, focusing on the scene from one of your favourite daydreams earlier today. Continue to play in this scene as you fall asleep, and observe your hypnagogic state as long as you can.

Well done! You have completed another day of your journey. See you tomorrow morning for day 20.

Progressive Dreaming

Morning conscious dreamer! I hope last night's dream adventures were profound. Today, you are going to be learning about progressive dreaming and how you can revisit a dream from your past in order to carry on the adventure.

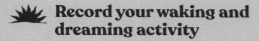

Record your waking and dreaming activity

Record your dreams from last night in your dream journal, your bedtime, rising time and total sleeping time from last night, and your wakening experience.

Schedule your reality checks

Schedule eight reality checks for today, including your dream symbol check.

What is progressive dreaming?

Have you ever experienced a dream that was really amazing, and just as it was about to reach a tense conclusion or moment of peak excitement... you wake up?

Perhaps you were inside a mysterious castle and as you were ascending the winding stairs, a sense of excitement started to build inside of you. You reach the top of the stairwell where there is a glowing yellow door, but just as you turn the handle to open it, you wake up! You are left with the feeling of missed opportunity and a sense of mystery.

This is a common but frustrating experience; what if there was a possibility to go back into the dream and carry on? Well, there is!

With a combination of practice, intent, imagination and hypnagogic observation, you can carry on with your dream adventures next time this occurs, and eventually, pick up a dream from where you left off long after the dream originally occurred.

Write the ending to a dream cut short

Read through your journal and find a dream that you awoke from too soon, and want to progress. Alternatively, if you have a striking memory of a dream from a long time ago that you'd like to revisit, you can use this.

In a quiet, comfortable place, spend ten minutes in silent reflection and play out what you remember of the dream in your mind like a film. When the dream reaches the point where it was originally interrupted, allow yourself to imagine the scene continuing. For example, you reach the top of the stairs of the castle and now you open the glowing yellow castle door. On the other side of the castle door is a world full of stars and planets. You then fly through the door and explore this dream galaxy.

As you sit, allow your mind to fill in the blanks to create a conclusion, then rewrite the dream with its new ending in your journal.

 Share the new ending to your incomplete dream, and a photo that represents a part of your dream.

Bedtime and dream tea ritual

Begin the bedtime checklist from day 4, three hours before bedtime. Prepare your dream tea to take to bed with you.

 ## Revisit the dream that you want to progress

As you drift off to sleep, imagine yourself stepping back into the dream that you focused on progressing earlier. Play the dream from the beginning, and continue to expand and explore the ending as you fall asleep.

Great work! You have completed day 20 of your journey. I hope that your dreams are progressive and wholesome tonight. See you tomorrow morning for day 21.

Dream Sharing

Good morning conscious dreamer! I hope that your dreams were rich last night.

You've been journeying through your dreams as a conscious dreamer for three weeks now, and it'd be a shame for you to keep all of these amazing nightly experiences to yourself.

Actively sharing your dreams with others can assist with dream interpretation, your dream memory recall and also with triggering more dreams. It can be fun and helpful to have a dream buddy or a group of dreamer friends that you can share dreams with. So today you will begin to explore the art of dream sharing!

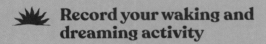 Record your waking and dreaming activity

Record your dreams from last night in your dream journal, your bedtime, rising time and total sleeping time from last night, and your wakening experience.

Schedule your reality checks

Schedule eight reality checks for today, including your dream symbol check.

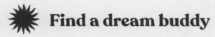

Find a dream buddy

Contact a friend or family member that you feel comfortable sharing your dreams with and ask them if they would like to share dreams with you. Let your intuition guide you towards the right dream buddy!

After you've found your dream buddy, have a go at interpreting each other's dreams. Did your buddy notice anything about your dream that you didn't? Write down any insight or clarity that came from your companion's interpretation of your dream below:

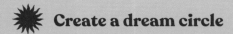 **Create a dream circle**

Another way of sharing dreams is to start or join a dream circle. A dream circle is a safe place where you can meet up with other dreamers to share dreams, ideas, techniques, theories and tips about becoming more conscious dreamers.

You can start a dream circle with a few friends in your own home, a community venue or a public park.

Write down the names of four to ten friends to invite to your dream circle:

Dreamer 1
....

Dreamer 2
....

Dreamer 3
....

Dreamer 4
....

Dreamer 5
....

Dreamer 6
....

Dreamer 7
....

Dreamer 8
....

Dreamer 9
....

Dreamer 10
....

Write down where you are going to meet:

Venue
....

Commit to a consistent schedule. How often are you going to meet, and when is your first meeting?

We will meet every
....

Our first meeting will be on
....

Commit to a length of time (a minimum of two hours gives you enough time to share and explore):

Our session will last for
....

Announce to your chosen friends that you are organizing a dream circle.

When the time comes for your dream circle to meet, revisit this book and follow the steps on the next page.

How to lead your dream circle

- Commit to recording your dreams in your journals before your session, and bring these along to the circles for sharing and discussion.
- Create a peaceful and comfortable space for your circle. You can sit in a circle on the floor, or on comfortable furniture. Candles, tea and aromatherapy oils can help create a calming environment for sharing dreams.
- Open the circle by introducing yourself and sharing a dream. It could be a dream from the previous night, or perhaps a profound dream from previous years that left a lasting impression on you.
- Discuss and explore each other's dreams, being sure to keep things moving around the circle.
- Use your notebook to make notes during your dream-sharing session. Feel free to draw, scribble and note down anything that interests you.
- At the end of the sessions, set dream tasks and goals before organizing your next session.

Connect with other dreamers in the online conscious dreamer community. Find a dream you would like to share and post it with a photo that resembles your dream, or a video of yourself recounting your dream. Then, search the hashtag and look at other conscious dreamers' dreams to see if any are similar to yours.

Bedtime and dream tea ritual

Begin the bedtime checklist from day 4, three hours before bedtime. Prepare your dream tea to take to bed with you.

Revisit your intention

As you fall asleep, repeat your intention to yourself ten times, observing your hypnagogic state as long as you can.

Fantastic work! You've completed the third week of your journey. I hope you're feeling proud of your progress. See you tomorrow morning for day 22.

PART IV:
Integrating

Dreamwork

Good morning, conscious dreamer!

Welcome to the final leg of your conscious dreaming journey, where all of your hard work over the last few weeks will begin to come together. For this final phase, you will be learning how to integrate everything you've learned over the past few weeks into your life as you prepare to move on to a new phase of your conscious dreaming practice outside of this book.

We will begin the integration process through the practice of dreamwork. But first, complete your usual morning activities.

Record your waking and dreaming activity

Record your dreams from last night in your dream journal, your bedtime, rising time and total sleeping time from last night, and your wakening experience.

Schedule your reality checks and W.I.L.D. meditation

Schedule eight reality checks for today, including your dream symbol check.

Set aside 20 minutes today to practise your W.I.L.D. meditation, and focus on exploring any dream scenes that you are trying to germinate.

Dreamwork

Dreamwork is about decoding the unconscious messages and lessons in your dreams, and incorporating them into your waking consciousness. It involves learning to understand your unique dream language, such as understanding the dream symbols you began to analyze last week.

Dreamwork is like homework. Like school, your dreams can teach you many things. If you do your dreamwork daily and consistently, you can gain deep insight and understanding from your dreams that can help you in your waking life.

On the next page is a dreamwork routine to help you decode and learn from your dreams. You might like to begin practising this every day straight after you record a dream, or revisit it in the evening when you have had the day to reflect upon its potential meaning. Use your intuition as to when to do your dreamwork, as some dreams take longer to untangle than others.

Practise your dreamwork

1 Read back through your dream journal and choose a dream that you haven't yet analyzed in this book.

2 Write the title of the dream on a piece of paper. For example, The Girl Who Was Chased by a Bear on her Way to a Tea Party

3 Then, list an object or dream character that appears in your dream.

4 Now, reimagine your dream from the perspective of that object or dream character. For example, if you were to imagine you were the bear in this scenario, you might write: 'I was lost on my way to a tea party in the woods, and worried about missing out on the fun. I saw a white rabbit and a girl running past with a tasty cake so I ran with her to the party.'

5 How does this new version differ? Write down your discoveries, and remember that each part of the dream is you. Seeing each symbol, object or dream character as being an aspect of you can help reveal the lessons the dream is trying to get through to you.

6 Record the lessons you have learned through this new version of the dream. For example, 'I have learned that I am worried about missing out on the fun parts of life, and have a misunderstood side to me that wants to be acknowledged.'

7 Re-title your dream inspired by the twist of this new version. For example, The Lost Bear and the Tea Party.

8 Now that you are acquainted with this dreamwork technique, practise it on two more dreams from your dream journal on separate pieces of paper.

 Share one of your dreams from the activity above with an image that represents it.

Bedtime and dream tea ritual

Begin the bedtime checklist from day 4, three hours before bedtime. Prepare your dream tea to take to bed with you.

 Revisit your W.I.L.D. meditation

As you fall asleep, see if you can revisit the scene you visited in your W.I.L.D. meditation earlier today. Observe your hypnagogic state as long as you can and try to remain focused on this scene as you drift into sleep.

Great work! You have completed day 22 of your journey and have begun the process of integrating your dreaming experiences into your waking life.

See you tomorrow for day 23.

Embodying Your Dreams

Rise and shine, conscious dreamer!

Today you will focus on embodying your dreams. Embodying your dreams is the act of following positive guidance from your dreams in your waking life. For example, you have a dream that you were confidently speaking to a room full of people, and you decide to embody your behaviour in your dream by overcoming your shyness in waking life by practising your public speaking.

Embodying the positive guidance from your dreams can be deeply transformative, inspiring and can help to enrich your life, so prepare to think positively, and begin benefiting from your dreams today.

Record your waking and dreaming activity

Record your dreams from last night in your dream journal, your bedtime, rising time and total sleeping time from last night, and your wakening experience.

Practise your dreamwork underneath today's dream in your journal, or leave some space to revisit it later.

Schedule your reality checks

Schedule eight reality checks for today, including your dream symbol check.

Reflect on your most profound dreams

Read through all of the dreams that you have recorded in your journal, and select a dream that had a profound impact on you.

Title the dream if you haven't already, and write down its name below.

....

....

Now, note down what insight, lessons or inspiration can be gained from these dreams. For example, you have a dream that you and your friends have transformed into brightly coloured balloons, and are bobbing up and down in the sky. You wake up laughing and in a good mood. The guidance you receive from this dream is to laugh and be more lighthearted.

....

....

....

....

....

....

....

....

....

....

....

Finally, note down if you observed any changes in your waking behaviour after experiencing these profound dreams. If you didn't, note down any emotions that are stirred up when you recollect these dreams and reflect on what they could mean.

For example, 'This dream made me feel good, and ever since, I have made a more conscious effort to laugh and be more silly and lighthearted.' Or, 'When I remember this dream, I feel longing, which implies that inviting more laughter into my life could benefit me positively.'

Embody your dreams in your waking life

Using your reflections above, set yourself a task to carry out which could help you integrate the lessons you learned from your dreams into your life.

For example, if your dreams are telling you that you are in need of a little more fun and laughter in your life, set yourself a goal to do something that embodies this.

Set your task or goal here, and if possible, a deadline to have completed it by:

....

....

....

....

....

....

....

....

....

....

....

....

....

Deadline:
....

 Share a photo of your task with a timestamp from today, and some words about what you are trying to embody in your waking life.

Bedtime and dream tea ritual

Begin the bedtime checklist from day 4, three hours before bedtime. Prepare your dream tea to take to bed with you.

 Repeat your intention

As you fall asleep, recite your intention to yourself. Observe your hypnagogic state as long as you can as you drift into sleep.

Amazing work! Day 23 of your journey is complete.
See you tomorrow morning for day 24.

Personal Mythology

Good morning, conscious dreamer!

Today you will continue your journey of integration by working with the symbols and imagery that you've gathered from your dreams to create your own personal mythology.

Your personal mythology is your fundamental story, and is layered with meaning, symbols, narratives and emotions. The process of developing your own personal mythology can be very creative, healing and empowering, because it requires you to ask existential questions about your identity, such as 'Who am I and what is my purpose?'

So, complete your regular morning exercises, and then let's get started with bringing your personal mythology to life!

 ## Record your waking and dreaming activity

Record your dreams from last night in your dream journal, your bedtime, rising time and total sleeping time from last night, and your wakening experience.

Practise your dreamwork underneath today's dream in your journal, or leave some space to revisit it later.

 ## Schedule your reality checks

Schedule eight reality checks for today, including your dream symbol check.

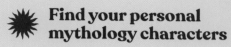

Find your personal mythology characters

For this activity, you are going to imagine that your dreaming and waking life is like a film. In each of these parts of your life, you are the leading actor, and you fit into one of the roles listed.

Angel

Hero/Heroine

Artist   Samaritan

Child   Hedonist

Magician   Shape shifter

Rebel   Survivor

Scientist   Mystic

Lover   Healer

Warrior

Villain

Peacemaker

Trickster   Spirit

Rescuer   Animal

Victim   Adventurer

Other

Achiever   Detective

Vampire   Athlete

Warrior   Seeker

Ruler   Teacher

Mystic

Think about the dreams you have been logging. Write down which role best describes your dreaming self, and give yourself a name.

....
....
....
....
....

Think about the events in your waking life. Which role best describes your waking self?

....
....
....
....
....

Which role do you aspire to be in your waking life? Give this character a name.

....
....
....
....
....

 ## Write your own mythology

On a piece of paper, write a story that will become part of your own personal mythology. At the centre of this story is tthe character that you aspire to be in your waking life. Get creative and write a short story or myth about this character, making it as abstract as you like. Consider the areas of your waking life that you would like to improve, and imagine your aspirational character making these improvements through the story. Incorporate any recurring themes, emotions, symbols, objects, animals and people that you have noticed in your dreams into your stories.

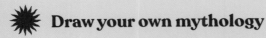 **Draw your own mythology**

Finally, draw the character that you created in your story below, surrounded by the symbols from your dreams that you have integrated into your new personal mythology, and their name. You can visualize your aspirational waking character and tell yourself your story any time you need a boost of motivation or confidence.

 Share a picture of your aspirational waking character, and some details of the mythology you created for it.

Bedtime and dream tea ritual

Begin the bedtime checklist from day 4, three hours before bedtime. Prepare your dream tea to take to bed with you.

 ## W.I.L.D meditation

Take 20 minutes before bedtime to practise your W.I.L.D. meditation, using this opportunity to imagine yourself as the aspirational waking character you wrote a personal mythology for earlier today. Try to remain focused on this scene as you drift into sleep.

Great work! Day 24 of your journey is complete. Have inspired dreaming tonight! See you tomorrow for day 25.

Dream Bridging

Good morning, conscious dreamer! I hope that your late-night W.I.L.D. meditation has left you feeling inspired.

Yesterday you created your own personal mythology as a way of putting the complex words of your dreams into a story. Today you will carry on connecting your dreams to your waking reality with a bit of dream bridging.

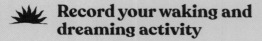

Record your waking and dreaming activity

Record your dreams from last night in your dream journal, your bedtime, rising time and total sleeping time from last night, and your wakening experience.

Practise your dreamwork underneath today's dream in your journal, or leave some space to revisit it later.

Schedule your reality checks

Schedule eight reality checks for today, including your dream symbol check.

Dream bridging

Dream bridging is the process of creating a bridge between your dreams and waking life. As a conscious dreamer, bridging your dream content can be beneficial for a variety of reasons: it can help you to find healing, creativity, guidance, adventure and of course, can help you integrate what you learn from your dreams into your waking life. You can create dream bridges by carrying out actions during your day that correlate with the content of your dreams.

For example, dream bridging can look like this:

- You have a dream set in your local park, so you decide to bridge the dream by planning a trip there later.
- You hear a song you know in a dream, so you take the time to sit quietly and listen to it during the day.
- You meet a friend in a dream, so you visit or talk to them.
- You notice that a recurring and comforting dream sign of yours is an owl, so you paint a picture of an owl and hang it on your wall.

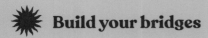 # Build your bridges

Now let's see which dreams you can bridge!

You can create a dream bridge the day after you've experienced a dream or, for dreams that include recurring locations, people or signs, you can create a dream bridge over time by repeating an activity.

Read through your dream journal and list any content that represents something that you would like to cross over your dream bridge into your waking life on a piece of paper. This content can include objects, places and dream signs.

Now, choose one of the things off your list and begin to make a plan for building your dream bridge. For example, 'I will write the lyrics to a tune I hear in my dreams that tells me I should welcome more music into my life. Once I have done this, I will sing it every day.' Finally, set yourself a task to complete today that will help you begin to construct your bridge. If you choose a long-term goal that will require time and planning – such as travelling to another country that you visit in your dreams, or getting a tattoo of a dream sign – set yourself a small task that you can achieve today, such as beginning to do some research.

 Share a photo of this bridge and some words about the dream bridge that you are constructing.

Bedtime and dream tea ritual

Begin the bedtime checklist from day 4, three hours before bedtime. Prepare your dream tea to take to bed with you.

 ## Repeat your intention

As you fall asleep, recite your intention to yourself. Observe your hypnagogic state as long as you can and try to remain focused on this scene as you drift into sleep.

Well done! You have accomplished day 25 of your journey. I hope that your dreams tonight are conscious and connected. See you tomorrow morning for day 26.

Record your waking and dreaming activity

Record your dreams from last night in your dream journal, your bedtime, rising time and total sleeping time from last night, and your wakening experience.

Practise your dreamwork underneath today's dream in your journal, or leave some space to revisit it later.

 ## Schedule your reality checks

Schedule eight reality checks for today, including your dream symbol check.

Build your dream altar

Your dream altar should be personal to you and you can make it as creative or minimal as you like. It can be located close to your bed or elsewhere in your bedroom, but wherever you choose to build it, it should be a place that feels reflective and calming for you. Once you have created it, you can use your dream altar at night when you are setting your intent, and in the morning when you reflect and write in your dream journal.

To begin assembling your dream altar, choose and prepare your space. It doesn't have to be a big space, just a small area that you can dedicate specifically to your dreamwork.

Then, gather your dreaming tools and arrange them in your space. These tools can include:

- Your dream journal
- Dream herbs and plants
- Dream objects
- Images of personal dream symbols
- Personal mythology objects.

Other creative things that you may like to include on your altar are:

- Fairy lights
- Mood lights
- Candles
- Stones or crystals
- Essential oils or incense
- Drawings or artwork of your dreams.

Your dream altar is a reflection of you, so express yourself and have fun creating your altar!

 Share a photo of your dream altar.

Bedtime and dream tea ritual

Begin the bedtime checklist from day 4, three hours before bedtime. Prepare your dream tea to take to bed with you and take the time to reflect on your intention near your new dream altar.

 ## Repeat your intention

As you fall asleep, recite your intention to yourself. Observe your hypnagogic state as long as you can and try to remain focused on this scene as you drift into sleep.

Well done today! You have completed day 26 of your journey. I hope that your dreams are full of adventure and insight tonight. See you tomorrow morning for day 27.

Reflection

Good morning, conscious dreamer! How was your dreaming last night?
Part of putting the dream integration process into action is mastering the art of reflection. Today, you will be revisiting your original intent and taking stock of the dream material you have produced, and observations you have made on your journey. Today is important, because reflecting on everything you have produced and learned so far will provide you with the tools to better understand and improve yourself moving forward.

 ## Record your waking and dreaming activity

Record your dreams from last night in your dream journal, your bedtime, rising time and total sleeping time from last night, and your wakening experience.
Practise your dreamwork underneath today's dream in your journal, or leave some space to revisit it later.

 ## Schedule your reality checks

Schedule eight reality checks for today, including your dream symbol check.

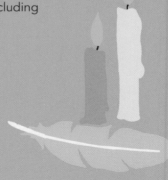

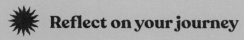 **Reflect on your journey**

Sit near your dream altar, reflect on the questions below and take the time to really think about them before writing down your answers.

What have you learned about yourself during this journey?

....
....
....
....
....
....

Has anything surprised you during your journey?

....
....
....
....
....
....

What have you enjoyed about it?

....
....
....
....
....
....

What have you found challenging?

....
....
....
....
....
....
....

How have your dreams evolved?

....
....
....
....
....
....
....

How has your original intention evolved since the beginning of this book and has it started to manifest?

....
....
....
....
....
....
....

Bedtime and dream tea ritual

Begin the bedtime checklist from day 4, three hours before bedtime. Prepare your dream tea to take to bed with you.

 ## Repeat your intention

As you fall asleep, recite your intention to yourself. Observe your hypnagogic state as long as you can and try to remain focused on this scene as you drift into sleep.

 Share a photo of your favourite illustration in this book and some words about what you have learnt during your dream journey so far

Well done! You have accomplished day 27 of your journey. Have magical dreams tonight! See you tomorrow morning for day 28.

Integration Ritual

Good morning, conscious dreamer!
I hope that this past week of integration has helped you gain a deeper understanding of yourself. Today you will be using an integration ritual to help you further absorb the insight that you gained from your day of reflection yesterday.
An integration ritual is a series of actions performed to help you bring together the insight that you've learned from your dreams. Creating a ritual for yourself will allow you to delve deeper into your reflection, and is a chance to honour yourself and to feel the transformative effects of all the conscious dreaming work that you've been engaging in for these past weeks.

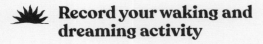 ## Record your waking and dreaming activity

Record your dreams from last night in your dream journal, your bedtime, rising time and total sleeping time from last night, and your wakening experience.
Practise your dreamwork underneath today's dream in your journal, or leave some space to revisit it later.

 ## Schedule your reality checks

Schedule eight reality checks for today, including your dream symbol check.

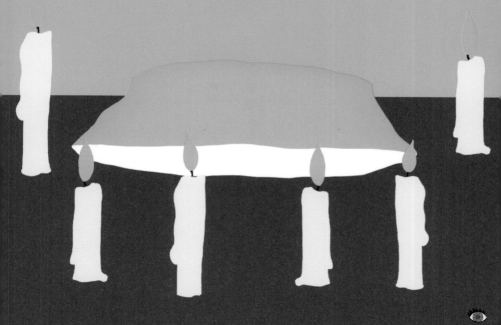

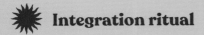 **Integration ritual**

Set aside 15 minutes for yourself today to carry out your integration ritual. You can carry it out in the morning or evening – just make sure that you are at home with access to your dream altar. When you are ready to begin your ritual, follow the steps below:

1 Sit comfortably at your dream altar. You might want to light a candle or create some mood lighting to get into the zone.

2 Read through all you have written in this book and consider the themes, insight, guidance or lessons that have come up for you during your journey through this book.

3 Read your answers to yesterday's questions out loud. Voicing what you've learned out loud helps you to bridge your understanding from your unconscious to your waking consciousness.

4 Then, sit in quiet meditation allowing your spoken words to help integrate your insights, taking deep breaths in through your nose and releasing out through your mouth.

5 Continue this way, focusing your awareness on your breath and the present moment.

6 If you notice any swelling emotions, simply allow them to rise and pass.

After your 15 minutes has concluded, consider what you would like to take from your integration ritual. Then, write yourself a short affirmation that you can repeat to yourself in the future any time you need to.

....

....

....

 Share a photo of your affirmation and some words about your integration ritual experience.

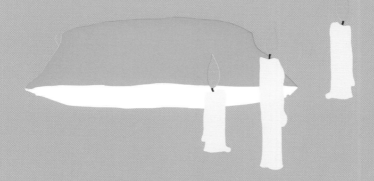

 Bedtime and dream tea ritual

Begin the bedtime checklist from day 4 three hours before bedtime. Prepare your dream tea to take to bed with you and reflect on your intent at your dream altar.

 Repeat your intention and affirmation

As you fall asleep, recite your intention to yourself, and the affirmation you created for yourself after your integration ritual. Observe your hypnagogic state as long as you can and try to remain focused on this scene as you drift into sleep.

Day 28 of your journey is complete. See you tomorrow morning for your penultimate day, day 29!

DAY 29

Showcase Your Dreamwork

Good morning, conscious dreamer.

You are nearly at the end of your journey! You've worked very hard throughout this guide and today you will put together a display to showcase your dreamwork.

Showcasing your work will not only help better integrate the results from your journey into your waking life, but it's also a chance to share and connect with other conscious dreamers. And as you learned in your third week, dream sharing is an amazing way to process your dreams and build connections with others.

Your showcase is the creative expression of your accumulative journey through this book, so allow your dreams to be your muse, and have fun today!

 Record your waking and dreaming activity

Record your dreams from last night in your dream journal, your bedtime, rising time and total sleeping time from last night, and your wakening experience.

Practise your dreamwork underneath today's dream in your journal, or leave some space to revisit it later.

 Schedule your reality checks

Schedule eight reality checks for today, including your dream symbol check.

Prepare your conscious dreamer showcase

Before you begin to create your showcase, think about how you would like to present your dreamwork. You might like to set your showcase up like an art gallery, film a tour of your work, record yourself discussing it or simply just arrange all your dreamwork on your bedroom floor. Get creative and do whatever feels intuitive to you. When you are ready to begin, follow the steps below:

1   With pen and paper, coloured pens, or paint, create a sign that reads: 'I AM A CONSCIOUS DREAMER'.

2   Choose where you would like to set up your showcase. It can be in your bedroom, elsewhere in your home, outside, or somewhere that you dream about with sentimental value.

3   Go to your dream altar and gather all of your dreamwork, including your new sign. Collect any dream recall objects, dream maps or notes that you have around your house that you have created during this journey.

4   If the intention you set yourself at the beginning of this journey included something like creating a painting, writing a song or beginning to develop a project, think about how you can incorporate this work into your showcase.

5   Assemble your showcase, taking as much time as you like.

6   Once it is complete, share your showcase with your friends and family. You can invite them to experience it in person, or you can send them a recording, photo or video of your work.

7   Let your achievements over the last month sink in as you take a quiet moment to observe your showcase. If your showcase is a physical display, you can leave it assembled for as long as you like.

8   Place your 'I AM A CONSCIOUS DREAMER' sign somewhere that you will be able to see it every day. This will serve as a reminder to you of your journey, and the success you have achieved from it.

   Share a photo of yourself with your 'I AM A CONSCIOUS DREAMER' sign, and any recordings from your showcase.

 ## Bedtime and dream tea ritual

Begin the bedtime checklist from day 4, three hours before bedtime. Prepare your dream tea to take to bed with you and take the time to reflect on your journey.

 ## Repeat your intention

As you fall asleep, think about what has made you proud during your journey through this book. Observe your hypnagogic state as long as you can as you drift into sleep.

Fantastic work! You have completed day 29 of your journey. See you tomorrow morning for day 30 – the final day of this part of your conscious dreaming journey!

DAY 30

Celebrate

Good morning conscious dreamer. I hope that your dreams were incredible last night. Welcome to the final day of your 30-day conscious dreaming journey!

It's important to reward yourself for all of the amazing work, discipline and dedication as a conscious dreamer these past 30 days, so today is a day of celebration. But before the party begins, make sure you carry out your usual morning activities. Carrying out these activities should be like second nature now, and it is important that you continue to do them every day. The responsibility is in your hands to keep your practice flourishing!

Record your waking and dreaming activity

Record your dreams from last night in your dream journal, your bedtime, rising time and total sleeping time from last night, and your wakening experience.

Practise your dreamwork underneath today's dream in your journal, or leave some space to revisit it later.

Schedule your reality checks

Schedule eight reality checks for today, including your dream symbol check.

You made it, conscious dreamer!

Congratulations on completing your 30-day journey! You've made it to the end, so fill out your Conscious Dreamer Certificate! Then, cut out this page and put your certificate somewhere you can see it every day.

Certificate

This certificate is awarded to:

....

for completing your 30-day conscious dreaming journey

Congratulations!
You are now a

Conscious Dreamer

 Share a photo of your Conscious Dreamer certificate with some words about the final day of your journey.

Be proud and thankful

You've worked hard over the past 30 days, so now is the time to reap the rewards!

Make a pledge below to do something you enjoy today to thank yourself for your hard work. It doesn't have to be dream related, just something that brings you joy in your waking life. Give yourself permission to have fun and be proud!

Look forward to the future

Finally, as this leg of your journey draws to a close, it's time to set a new statement of intent for yourself as you move into your next phase of evolution as a conscious dreamer.

Think about what you would like to focus on improving in your conscious dreaming practice moving forward, and what you would like to take with you from this journey.

Then below, set yourself a new intention to carry forward into your new life beyond this book. Use coloured pencils, pens and anything else you like to make it an inspiring piece. Once you're done, you might like to take a photo of it save it as a background on your phone or computer, where you can see it every day.

Bedtime and dream tea ritual

Begin the bedtime checklist from day 4, three hours before bedtime. Prepare your dream tea to take to bed with you and take the time to reflect on your new intention, and all the achievements you have accomplished over the last 30 days.

 ## Repeat your intention

As you fall asleep, recite your new intention to yourself, observing your hypnagogic state as long as you can as you drift into sleep, and into the next stage of your journey as a conscious dreamer...

It has been wonderful to journey with you over this past month, conscious dreamer! Now it's time for me to say goodbye. I hope that you carry on with your practice and let it continue to enrich your life. The power is in your hands now to keep your practice evolving, as you yourself are constantly changing and growing. So good luck, sweet dreams, and goodnight! Perhaps one day, we will meet again in a dream...

Acknowledgments & Resources

This book is dedicated to Vico and the children of Generation Z and Generation Alpha.

We live in a multiverse of vast possibilities! Through a wonderful set of synchronicities, I have come to pen this book. Along the way there have been many people whose connections have brought a richness, playfulness and inspiration to my explorations as a conscious dreamer:

Chloe Murphy	Tannaz Oroumchi
Jenniffer ClarOscura	Francesca Veronesi
Anthony Peake	Travis Lawrence
Charlie Morley	Troy Vrolyk
Luis Solarat	She's Lost Control
Ray Fiala	The Lucid Hive
Samantha Treasure	The Psychedelic Society

And all of the wonderful people that I've guided through the years.

Additional suggested reading material

Dreams: How to Connect with your Dreams to Enrich your Life (Conscious Guide). By Tree Carr. Octopus Publishing, 2018.

The Infinite Mindfield: The Quest to Find the Gateway to Higher Consciousness. By Anthony Peake. Watkins Publishing Ltd., 2013.

Liminal Dreaming: Exploring Consciousness at the Edges of Sleep. By Jennifer Dumpert. North Atlantic Books, USA, 2019.

Lucid Dreaming Made Easy: A Beginner's Guide to Waking Up in Your Dreams. By Charlie Morley. Hay House, UK, 2018.

The Archetypes and the Collective Unconscious (Collected Works of C.G. Jung). By Carl Jung. Routledge, 2nd edition, 1991.